# THE BIRTHDAY
# OF A KING

*Study* by Judson Edwards
*Commentary* by Charles Bugg

Free downloadable Teaching Guide for this study available at
NextSunday.com/teachingguides

NextSunday Resources
6316 Peake Road
Macon, Georgia 31210-3960
1-800-747-3016
©2014 by NextSunday Resources
All rights reserved.

# TABLE OF CONTENTS

## The Birthday of a King

# HOW TO USE THIS STUDY

*NextSunday Resources* Adult Bible Studies are designed to help adults study Scripture seriously within the context of the larger Christian tradition and, through that process, find their faith renewed, challenged, and strengthened. We study the Scriptures because we believe they affect our current lives in important ways. Each study contains the following three components:

## Study Guide

Each study guide lesson is arranged in four movements:

*Reflecting* recalls a contemporary story, anecdote, example, or illustration to help us anticipate the session's relevance in our lives.

*Studying* is centered on giving the biblical material in-depth attention while often surrounding it with helpful insights from theology, ethics, church history, and other areas.

*Understanding* helps us find relevant connections between our lives and the biblical message.

*What About Me?* provides brief statements that help unite life issues with the meaning of the biblical text.

## Commentary

Each study guide lesson is accompanied by an additional, in-depth commentary on the biblical material. Written by a different author than the study guide, each commentary gives the opportunity for learners to approach the Scripture text from a separate but complementary viewpoint.

## Teaching Guide

In addition to the provided study guide and commentary, *NextSunday Resources* also provides a *free* downloadable teaching guide, available at NextSunday.com. Each teaching guide gives the teacher tools for focusing on the content of each study guide lesson through additional commentary and Bible background information. Through teacher helps and teaching options, each teaching guide also provides substance for variety and choice in the preparation of each lesson.

# STUDY INTRODUCTION

The first four lessons in this unit draw inspiration from a traditional interpretation of the Advent candles as the Prophets' Candle, the Bethlehem Candle, the Shepherds' Candle, and the Angels' Candle. The final lesson, which occurs after Advent, celebrates the theological meaning of Jesus' birth as described in the prologue to John's Gospel.

In the first lesson, taking our cue from the Prophets' Candle, we delve into some of the prophetic words about the Messiah in the book of Isaiah. As we study these Old Testament prophecies, we will ask ourselves, How is God present in my life—yesterday, today, and tomorrow?

In honor of the Bethlehem Candle, we move in the second lesson to the little town of Bethlehem, a most unexpected place to serve as the birthplace of the King. Through what unexpected sources might God want to bless us? As we think about ancient Bethlehem, we will ponder this question.

The third lesson reminds us of the Shepherds' Candle. Shepherds were considered untrustworthy and irreligious, so it is surprising that God chose shepherds to receive the news of Jesus' birth. We also may sometimes feel unworthy of God's love. The lesson invites us to think about the kinds of people God uses.

In the fourth lesson, we focus on the Angels' Candle and ponder the angel's difficult message to Mary. What hard thing might God call us to do?

Finally, in the fifth lesson we explore what it means that "the Word became flesh and lived among us" (Jn 1:14). We conclude our study by asking a practical question: How is the birth of Christ relevant to my life?

May these sessions help us celebrate with new meaning the birthday of the King.

# O COME, O COME, EMMANUEL

*Isaiah 7:10-17; 8:1-4, 19; 9:2-7*

## Central Question

How is God present in my life—yesterday, today, and tomorrow?

## Scripture

**Isaiah 7:10-17**  10  Again the LORD spoke to Ahaz, saying, 11  Ask a sign of the LORD your God; let it be deep as Sheol or high as heaven.  12  But Ahaz said, I will not ask, and I will not put the LORD to the test.  13  Then Isaiah said: "Hear then, O house of David! Is it too little for you to weary mortals, that you weary my God also?  14  Therefore the LORD himself will give you a sign. Look, the young woman is with child and shall bear a son, and shall name him Immanuel.  15  He shall eat curds and honey by the time he knows how to refuse the evil and choose the good. 16  For before the child knows how to refuse the evil and choose the good, the land before whose two kings you are in dread will be deserted.  17  The LORD will bring on you and on your people and on your ancestral house such days as have not come since the day that Ephraim departed from Judah—the king of Assyria."

**Isaiah 8:1-4**  1  Then the LORD said to me, Take a large tablet and write on it in common characters, "Belonging to Maher-shalal-hash-baz,"  2  and have it attested for me by reliable witnesses, the priest Uriah and Zechariah son of Jeberechiah.  3  And I went to the prophetess, and she conceived and bore a son. Then the LORD said to me, Name him Maher-shalal-hash-baz;  4  for before the child knows how to call "My father" or "My mother," the wealth of Damascus and the spoil of Samaria will be carried away by the king of Assyria.

**Isaiah 9:2-7** 2 The people who walked in darkness have seen a great light; those who lived in a land of deep darkness—on them light has shined. 3 You have multiplied the nation, you have increased its joy; they rejoice before you as with joy at the harvest, as people exult when dividing plunder. 4 For the yoke of their burden, and the bar across their shoulders, the rod of their oppressor, you have broken as on the day of Midian. 5 For all the boots of the tramping warriors and all the garments rolled in blood shall be burned as fuel for the fire. 6 For a child has been born for us, a son given to us; authority rests upon his shoulders; and he is named Wonderful Counselor, Mighty God, Everlasting Father, Prince of Peace. 7 His authority shall grow continually, and there shall be endless peace for the throne of David and his kingdom. He will establish and uphold it with justice and with righteousness from this time onward and forevermore. The zeal of the LORD of hosts will do this.

## *Reflecting*

Just after World War II, a Lutheran minister named Günter Rutenborn wrote a play titled *The Sign of Jonah*. The play, set in post-Hitler Germany, attempts to discover who is to blame for the awful atrocities of the Nazi regime.

Various characters—Hitler, the bureaucrats, the apathetic "average man," and even the Jews themselves—are suggested, but then a man gets up from the audience and strides on stage. He says that the real culprit is God; that God created a horrible world and then does nothing when evil runs rampant. At first, everyone is shocked at this audacious idea, but gradually the characters on stage begin to agree. They eventually form a jury and find God guilty as charged. God's punishment is to come and live in this horrible world.

Next, the three archangels—Gabriel, Michael, and Raphael—are dispatched to execute the sentence on God. Gabriel saunters onstage and declares that he wants God to be born in a cattle stall on the backside of nowhere with a peasant girl for a mother. And he wants God to be a Jew in a Jew-hating world. Michael comes onstage and says he wants God to experience constant frustration and to be misunderstood and even rejected by family and friends. Finally, Raphael enters and says that he wants God to experience extreme suffering and to die an agonizing death.

As the archangels exit the stage, the house lights go down, and all of a sudden it strikes those sitting in the dark theater that God has already served that sentence. In the person of Jesus, God became a human being and "walked a mile in our shoes." Yahweh became Immanuel—"God with us"—so that we would know forever that God understands who we are and what we experience.

> **?** How does believing in God as "Immanuel" affect our daily lives?

## Studying

When Matthew writes about the birth of Jesus, he quotes from the prophet Isaiah: "Look, the virgin shall conceive and bear a son, and they shall name him Immanuel" (Mt 1:23; see Isa 7:14). That passage from Isaiah 7 is the first of three passages in Isaiah that predict the birth of babies who will be significant to the people of Judah.

In Isaiah 7, the prophet confronts Ahaz, king of Judah, who has considered joining forces with Israel and Syria to battle Assyria. Isaiah warns against that alliance and tells Ahaz that a baby named Immanuel will soon be born, and before this baby knows right from wrong, Israel and Syria will be defeated. This Immanuel baby, in other words, was a symbol to Judah in the eighth century BC. Isaiah

> According to 2 Kings 16:1, Ahaz was 20 years old when he began to reign and reigned for 20 years. According to 2 Kings 18:2, Hezekiah was 25 years old when he began to reign. In other words, Hezekiah was born about 5 years before Ahaz became king. It is possible, however, that a copyist's error has crept into the text. If Hezekiah were not 25 but 20 upon his accession, he would have been born in the first year of Ahaz's reign—and thus possibly the "son" Isaiah foresaw during the Syro-Ephraimitic crisis of 735 BC.
>
> Another possibility is that the "son" of Isaiah 7 is Maher-shalal-hash-baz, the son of the prophet himself, who is explicitly named in Isaiah 8:1, 3. It is still possible, however, that Isaiah had Hezekiah son of Ahaz in mind in chapter 9.

uses the birth of this child to offer a word of warning and advice to King Ahaz.

In Isaiah 8, another baby is born. This one is Isaiah's own son. Isaiah gives him the strange name Maher-shalal-hash-baz, which means "the spoil speeds, the prey hastens." The baby's name gives Judah another warning: avoid alliances with Damascus and Syria, for they will soon become "spoil" and "prey" for the Assyrian Empire. Isaiah predicts that before this baby can say "Mama" and "Daddy," those places will experience the wrath of the Assyrians. Again, this child serves as a warning to Judah not to become entangled with other nations.

In Isaiah 9, the birth of a third child is proclaimed. This child is called "Wonderful Counselor, Mighty God, Everlasting Father, Prince of Peace." Some scholars believe this baby is a reference to Hezekiah, who would succeed Ahaz as king of Judah and lead the people in political and spiritual reform. Of the three births in Isaiah, this third one promises the most hope. This child will be a great light in the darkness who will establish a kingdom of peace.

Although all three of these births refer to babies born in Isaiah's own time, Matthew and other followers of Jesus through the centuries have seen the ultimate fulfillment of

> See, I and the children whom the LORD has given me are signs and portents in Israel from the LORD of hosts, who dwells on Mount Zion. (Isa 8:18)

Isaiah's prophecies in Jesus' birth some 700 years later. No one had truly fulfilled the prophesied role of Immanuel—until Jesus came. No one really merited the title of Wonderful Counselor, Mighty God, Everlasting Father, Prince of Peace—until Jesus showed up. People of faith read those old prophecies of Isaiah and declared, "Jesus measures up!"

As the early followers of Jesus reflected on his life, they saw in him all the qualities Isaiah described. They realized that Jesus was Immanuel. When they saw Jesus, they saw God. In a few Sundays, we will study John's poetic tribute to Jesus in the prologue to his Gospel. In exalted language, John declares, "And the Word became flesh and lived among us, and we have seen his glory, the glory as of a father's only son, full of grace and truth" (Jn 1:14).

The first generations of disciples also saw Jesus as the embodiment of Wonderful Counselor, Mighty God, Everlasting Father, and Prince of Peace. They saw Jesus as the one who came to establish an everlasting kingdom of love and peace.

Though we seldom connect Jesus to Isaiah's son, Maher-shalal-hash-baz, perhaps it is possible that Jesus fulfills that name too. Jesus came to warn us about entanglements with people and projects that would stifle our purpose and dilute our commitment to God.

Gustave Doré, *The Prophet Isaiah*

This we know for certain: 700 years before Jesus, Isaiah prophesied about the births of three boys. Those boys had a message for Judah and served as signs to the people. Is it any wonder that 700 years later people connected these Scriptures with Jesus? They heard of the birth of a baby boy, watched him grow to manhood, listened to his profound teachings, observed his life of love and servanthood, saw him die on a cruel cross, and then were amazed at his miraculous resurrection. They knew this was no ordinary man. This was Isaiah's Immanuel—the Wonderful Counselor, Mighty God, Everlasting Father, Prince of Peace. This was the one Israel had anticipated for centuries.

## Understanding

Our newspaper recently told the story of a church theft in which someone stole the statue of Jesus from the sanctuary. The only problem was that no one knew for certain when it was stolen. Evidently the people of the church grew so accustomed to the statue that they viewed it merely as a piece of furniture. For all anyone knew, Jesus could have been missing for days.

How can we keep the Christmas story from becoming too familiar to us?

It's easy to take Jesus for granted, often especially at Christmas. We know the stories, carols, and traditions, and we certainly know that Jesus was born in a manger in Bethlehem. But despite our familiarity with the story, the proclamation of the Bible about Jesus is astonishing: He was God-in-the flesh. He was born like those baby boys Isaiah prophesied about, and he grew up to be Immanuel and the Prince of Peace.

The implications of the incarnation for our lives are astonishing as well. No longer must we wonder "what God looks like." God looks like Jesus, thinks like Jesus, and loves like Jesus. Jesus is Immanuel, "God with us."

No longer must we wonder if God understands our situation. Now we know: in Jesus, God truly "walked a mile in our shoes." When we suffer, grieve, feel betrayed and forsaken, and come face to face with our own death, we know God has been there because Jesus has been there. As the play *The Sign of Jonah* dramatically showed, God has served that sentence and knows what it's like to be human. Yahweh has become Immanuel, and our understanding *of* God and appreciation *for* God will never be the same.

## What About Me?

- *This is a good time to be grateful for Jesus.* As we celebrate his birth this year, let's express thanks for some of his qualities—his keen insight into life, his love for "the least of these," his courage in the face of opposition, his willingness to die—that mean most to us.

- *Love is always "particular."* To love the world, God had to become one man in one place and time. Love is always specific. We can't love the world; we can only love particular people in the world. The incarnation reminds us that love thinks small. We will revisit this truth when we study the prologue to John's Gospel in the last session in this unit.

- *Communication is an inside job.* To communicate with humanity, God had to become a human being. Even God couldn't lob truths from afar. This fact has many implications for the way we communicate with others. Like God, we have to identify with individuals before we can hope to influence them.

- *Jesus is the best picture we have of God.* Matthew quoted Isaiah about the baby named Immanuel because he saw the fulfillment of that name in Jesus. Jesus was "God with us" and gave us the best revelation of God we've ever seen. It has been said that Jesus was God's way of getting rid of a bad reputation. If we're ever tempted to believe in a bad God, remembering Jesus will bring us back to the truth.

# O COME, O COME, EMMANUEL

*Isaiah 7:10-17; 8:1-4, 19; 9:2-7*

## Introduction

On my way to the office, I pass a small frame house. A sign in front of the house identifies the resident as a "psychic." A larger sign says that for a mere five dollars, I can get my palm read and hear my future.

This morning I looked in the newspaper and saw the astrological readings. I did look at my sign, but only for the sake of this lesson and to make a point! By the way, this is not going to be a good day for me, so maybe I should go back to bed.

Many people are interested in knowing the future. The psychic palm reader; the astrological readings in the newspaper; books like Hal Lindsey's *The Late Great Planet Earth*, or the recently popular *Left Behind* series by Tim LaHaye and Jerry Jenkins—all of these things remind us that people are hungry to know the "not yet."

Mention the word "prophecy" in relation to the Bible and many people envision God opening the curtain to the future and letting us see what will be. To some extent, this view of the prophets is true, but there is more. J. F. A. Sawyer reminds us that to prophesy is "to speak for or on behalf of someone" ("Immanuel," *The New Interpreter's Dictionary of the Bible*, vol. 4 [Nashville: Abingdon, 2009] 622). With reference to our lesson, Isaiah was speaking in the early part of his prophetic ministry to a specific crisis in the southern kingdom. The nation of Judah wondered whether they should forge military and political alliances to protect themselves from external threats or simply trust Yahweh (631).

While the prophet was not specifically speaking of events that would occur more than 700 years after the time of his writing, Isaiah *was* speaking about the ways in which God works. In that sense, the prophet creates anticipation about what Yahweh will do in the future. Centuries later, the early followers of Christ looked back at these words and were reminded of the surprising ways in which the Holy One works.

## The The God Who Is With Us Tomorrow

The word "advent" is derived from a Latin word that means "to come." For Christians, this word reminds us that God has come into the world, is seeking to come or to be born in us now, and will come again. When God in Christ comes again, God will consummate history and prevail over the forces of evil. (For a simple and excellent discussion of Advent and the seasons of the Christian year, see Douglas E. Wingeier, ed., *Keeping Holy Time: Studying the Revised Common Lectionary*, Year C [Nashville: Abingdon, 2003].)

Interestingly, many of the New Testament readings during Advent begin with words about the *second* coming of Jesus. Why? For many of us, the idea of Jesus' second advent is problematic. Apocalyptic books like Revelation or apocalyptic texts like 1 Thessalonians 5:1-11, which convey the belief that while present circumstances are bad, God and God's people will ultimately prevail, have given rise to questionable ideas such as the rapture or the tribulation.

When my daughter was young, she visited a friend whose parents had a large picture of the so-called "rapture"—a word, by the way, that is never used in the Bible. The picture showed people flying out of cars or rising from the cemetery while other folks crashed into each other's automobiles and generally had a bad time.

The message of the picture was obvious. Follow Jesus, and you will go to heaven at the rapture. Don't follow Jesus, and you are left behind.

For weeks Laura Beth had questions and fears about the picture. "Daddy, is this the way God works? How do I know that I'm going to heaven? Why do the people who are ascending look so happy while some of their family and friends are smashing into telephone poles?"

As her parents, all Diane and I knew to do was keep her from going to that friend's house again. Obviously, she was too young for a lecture on the nature of apocalyptic literature and how we should read it not literally, but as a reminder to the Christian community that in the final analysis, God will prevail.

Advent begins with the message that God is the God of tomorrow. God will come again not so we can get into arguments about whether the tribulation occurs before the rapture or when the battle of Armageddon will be fought.

The message of the second coming is to create anticipation and hope in Christians. The same God who has worked in history and is working in history will continue to work in history to effect God's purposes.

Thus, we view Isaiah not as God's psychic but as God's prophet. A prophet sees the pattern of Yahweh's work and reminds all of us that God is with us (Immanuel). The prophet understands that God works through the powerless in order that God's power will be manifest.

When Isaiah writes, "For a child has been born for us, a son given to us" (v. 6), the Christian preacher sees this and may certainly apply it to the way God reveals himself in Jesus. Yet, it is the same way that God has always worked. It is Yahweh's pattern. Of all the nations, God chose Israel to bless and to be a blessing. In terms of power and influence, Israel was a "helpless child."

When the nation was threatened by Assyria, Babylonia, or any of the other nations with mature military might, Yahweh wanted Israel to remember that the nation was dependent on the "God of Abraham, Isaac, and Jacob."

## The God Who Was With Us Yesterday

Christopher Seitz, in his commentary on First Isaiah, states, "The section of text stretching from 7:1–9:7 is the most important sustained block of tradition in the presentation of Isaiah 1–12" (*Isaiah 1–39*, Interpretation [Louisville: John Knox, 1993] 60). Seitz recognizes the issue of "Who Is Immanuel" (60–61). Offering suggestions that range from the names of one or more

of the prophet's own children to the traditional Christian interpretation that it is God coming as Jesus, Seitz attempts to place
these words in their proper historical context.

Ahaz was the king of Judah. Frankly, he was not the best
monarch. Threatened by the political machinations of Assyria
and an opposing coalition of Syria and Israel, the southern kingdom of Judah with its capital of Jerusalem was being pushed to
form military and political alliances to protect itself.

According to Isaiah 7:10, Yahweh spoke to Ahaz, but Ahaz did
not listen. At this point Isaiah speaks: "Hear then, O house of
David! Is it too little for you who weary mortals, that you weary
my God also?" (v. 13). At this point, the prophet begins to talk
about the sign from God, a young maiden who will bear a son.

While the names of the various nations and players in this
historical drama may be hard for us to remember, it is important
to note the fundamental message of Isaiah. Political leaders seek
to fashion military alliances in order to guard their interests, but
prophets remind us that ultimate security in life is found in relationship to the "God who is with us."

Several years ago, my wife gave me a porcelain figure of a
preaching minister. Diane said it reminded her of me because he
was holding his Bible in one hand and gesturing with the other
hand. So far, so good! I have been known to hold my Bible while I
gesture.

What bothered me, however, was the look on the minister's
face. He looked "out of it." He had a pious expression, as if he
had never been in touch with real life. "Is this what you think
about me?" I asked. Diane assured me that I was not out of it,
but that was the last porcelain figure I ever got from her.

Even so, prophets and preachers have a reputation for pious
oversimplifying. In a complex, complicated world of intrigue and
positioning for power, the prophet's message is, "God comes in
the innocence of a child, and that innocence is the sign." "Trust
in this God" becomes the mantra of the minister.

The advent of God in Jesus comes riding the wave of a God
who has chosen the unlikeliest patterns to do the most incredible
things. The message of history from a secular perspective is that
things happen, and those with the most ingenuity and human

power prevail. The message of salvation history is that God is at work in the most unexpected places through people who would never be picked first on anybody's team.

## The God Who Is With Us Today

One of my favorite authors is Walter Brueggemann. In one of his books, Brueggemann has a chapter on "The Transformative Potential of a Public Metaphor" (*Interpretation and Obedience: From Faithful Reading to Faithful Living* [Minneapolis: Fortress, 1991] 70–99). To be honest, the chapter has nothing to do with Advent, Christians, or even the word "Immanuel." But the title is fascinating because it reminds us that if we can experience and internalize the reality of certain words, that reality can be a transformational event.

Our faith has always had strong elements of memory and anticipation. We have a holy book that recounts stories, sayings, songs, and a host of other literary forms that remind us that God has been at work well before we were called into being. We remember Miriam and Moses, David and Deborah, and a host of other biblical figures. I'm indebted to people like Bob Payne, Reverend Folds, and Mrs. Miller, each of whom encouraged me in my journey of faith.

At the same time, I live with anticipation and hope. I don't have a clue when Jesus will return, but I have conducted countless funeral services assuring people that someone whom they loved is going Home.

But what about now? What about this present moment? Can Christ be born into the mangers of our lives so that new life is stirred and something transformative happens? Is it possible for the word "Immanuel" to engage our memories, empower our anticipation, and energize us for the living of our days and nights?

Several years ago I preached at a church in the Atlanta area. Following the service, an elderly man greeted me. He kept repeating, "I can't get over it. The Lord became a baby for me!" The man had tears in his eyes. I wanted to say, "It was just a Christmas sermon." Then it dawned on me. It was just a Christmas sermon!

# Notes

# Notes

# O LITTLE TOWN OF BETHLEHEM

*Micah 5:2-5a; Luke 2:1-7*

## Central Question

**Through what unexpected sources might God want to bless me?**

## Scripture

**Micah 5:2-5a**  2  But you, O Bethlehem of Ephrathah, who are one of the little clans of Judah, from you shall come forth for me one who is to rule in Israel, whose origin is from of old, from ancient days.  3  Therefore he shall give them up until the time when she who is in labor has brought forth; then the rest of his kindred shall return to the people of Israel.  4  And he shall stand and feed his flock in the strength of the LORD, in the majesty of the name of the LORD his God. And they shall live secure, for now he shall be great to the ends of the earth;  5a  and he shall be the one of peace.

**Luke 2:1-7**  1  In those days a decree went out from Emperor Augustus that all the world should be registered.  2  This was the first registration and was taken while Quirinius was governor of Syria.  3  All went to their own towns to be registered.  4  Joseph also went from the town of Nazareth in Galilee to Judea, to the city of David called Bethlehem, because he was descended from the house and family of David.  5  He went to be registered with Mary, to whom he was engaged and who was expecting a child.  6  While they were there, the time came for her to deliver her child.  7  And she gave birth to her firstborn son and wrapped him in bands of cloth, and laid him in a manger, because there was no place for them in the inn.

## Reflecting

Martin Luther once drew a distinction between "right-handed power" and "left-handed power." Right-handed power is direct, obvious, and forceful. It is a linebacker sacking a quarterback, a president vetoing a bill, or a millionaire buying a shopping mall. When we think of power, the right-handed variety usually comes to mind.

But there is also left-handed power. Left-handed power is indirect, subtle, and gentle. It is a woman teaching a child to read, a friend crying with someone who is grieving, or a man giving a bowl of soup to someone who is hungry. Left-handed power doesn't look like power at all—until you experience it! Then it seems like the most powerful force in the world.

The Christmas story is full of left-handed power. Think of the examples: God becoming a baby in a manger; God choosing Mary and Joseph as the parents; the baby born in a cattle stall because there was no room for him in the inn. All these details smack of left-handed power. To many, they aren't the "proper" way a powerful God should come to earth.

Even Bethlehem, the birthplace of Jesus, is an area of left-handed power. Bethlehem wasn't a large, influential city; it was a small village. Micah called it "one of the little clans of Judah" (5:2). Bethlehem's only claim to fame was that David was born there centuries earlier.

It's strange that Bethlehem was the Messiah's birthplace. But this simple village reminds us of the strange, paradoxical ways of God. As we study Bethlehem today, we will also think about the mysterious ways God has worked in history. Bethlehem reminds us that the God of the Bible has an affinity for left-handed power.

## Studying

Long before Jesus was born, the prophet Micah predicted that the messiah would be born in Bethlehem of Ephrathah. From that little village "shall come forth for me one who is to rule in Israel" (5:2). But this ruler would not come soon, Micah warned. Israel would be like a woman in labor, he said, awaiting the birth of her child. Israel would have to wait for the arrival of the messiah until all the people returned from exile in Babylon (5:3).

When the messiah did come, he would be like a shepherd who feeds his flock and gives the sheep security (5:4). He would usher in a kingdom of peace (5:5a). Micah's prophecy, given in a time of oppression under the Assyrian Empire, would have filled Israel's heart with hope and anticipation.

That prophecy was fulfilled when Jesus was born some 700 years later, and Luke gives us his famous account of the Messiah's birth in the second chapter of his Gospel. He carefully shows how Joseph and Mary came to Bethlehem to be counted in the census (or poll tax) decreed by the Roman emperor Augustus, who ruled from 27 BC–AD 14. Israelites had to return to their families' hometowns. Since Joseph was "descended from the house and family of David" (Lk 2:3), his hometown was Bethlehem. At this point in the story, Augustus calls all the shots. This man, Rome's first emperor, was celebrated in his own day as a divine savior whose reign marked the dawn of a new era. Virgil's *Aeneid* calls him "son of a god, who will once again establish the golden age" (Vinson, 58–59). Joseph and Mary apparently have no say in the matter; the right-handed power of the state prevails at every turn. As Vinson notes, "Thus far, this is a story about the powers that be, the emperors and their lackeys who depose rulers and send in tax collectors and who, if they wish, can cook up a crazy scheme to move Galilean carpenters around like checkers" (61).

> Gaius Vivius Maximus, Prefect of Egypt [says]: seeing that the time has come for the house to house census, it is necessary to compel all those who for any cause whatsoever are residing out of their provinces to return to their own homes, that they may both carry out the regular order of the census and may attend diligently to the cultivation of their allotments. (Egyptian provincial census decree, AD 104)

Augustus decided to register his entire domain, and for that reason alone, Joseph and Mary left Nazareth and made the eighty-mile trip to Bethlehem. Mary went into labor there and gave birth to her son.

Since Bethlehem was crowded with people gathering for the census, there were no rooms available, and Jesus' birth probably took place in a barn or cave. Then his mother put him in the animals' feeding trough. Talk about humble beginnings! And talk about left-handed power. Luke's birth narrative is left-handed from beginning to end. Think of the ingredients in the story: a frightened young woman pregnant out of wedlock, a confused carpenter, a couple frantically trying to find a birthing room, a newborn baby, a manger in a cattle stall. These elements equal the birth of the long-awaited king. What a surprising story, and what a necessary reminder of the way God often works.

Can you think of other examples of left-handed power?

In his *Interpretation* commentary on Micah, James Limburg writes,

> We recognize a biblical theme here: God's choice of the least likely, the littlest, to accomplish God's purpose. Thus Gideon declared himself to be from the weakest clan, and the youngest in his family (Judg. 6:15). Saul described his tribe as the "least" of those in Israel (1 Sam. 9:21). The Lord chose David, the youngest, over his brothers (1 Sam. 16:1-13). The theme finds climactic expression in the announcement that the Messiah and Savior of the world is the baby lying in the manger (Luke 2). (186)

Think for a moment about some of the other surprises in the Bible. Why would God choose a stuttering murderer like Moses to lead Israel out of bondage in Egypt? Why would God have Jonah swallowed by a giant fish? Why would God allow enemies to conquer Israel and Judah? Why would God choose such eccentric men to serve as prophets? Why would God choose to become a baby in a bed of straw? Why would God choose a peasant girl like Mary to give birth to the Messiah? Why would God let Jesus die on a cross? Why would God choose an angry persecutor of Christians like Saul of Tarsus to be the apostle to the Gentiles?

For my thoughts are not your thoughts, nor are your ways my ways. For as the heavens are higher than the earth, so are my ways higher than your ways and my thoughts higher than your thoughts. (Isaiah 55:8-9)

Why? Why? Why? The questions are endless, but the conclusion is obvious: God doesn't do things our way. God's ways seem strange to us. We would have done things differently. But when we read the Bible, we become aware that God does things God's way. We also see that God often chooses the Bethlehems, the Marys, and the Josephs of the world to do great things.

God takes delight in advancing the kingdom through humble people, small places, and ordinary events. Frequently in Scripture, God is left-handed.

## Understanding

Once we become familiar with the biblical story and realize how God has worked in history, we can make two simple assumptions. First, we can assume that God will bless us in unusual, unexpected, left-handed ways. We will go to Bethlehem more often than we know, and God will bless our lives through more Marys and Josephs than we can count.

Occasionally in the Bible, God is referred to as "the God of Abraham, Isaac, and Jacob" (for example, Exod 3:6). When we think about that designation, it tells more about God than we realize at first.

God is "the God of Abraham." Abraham is one of the superstars of Scripture, the founder of the people of Israel, and one of the heroes of faith listed in Hebrews 11. It's not surprising that God is the God of Abraham.

God is also "the God of Isaac." Isaac comes across in the Bible as a "nobody" who is known primarily as the son of Abraham and the father of Jacob. It's a little more surprising that God is the God of Isaac.

The real surprise is that God is "the God of Jacob." Jacob is a scoundrel and a con artist in Scripture, constantly cheating and conniving to get his way. Yet our God is the God of Jacob, too.

The chances are better than good that we will be touched and blessed by some "Jacobs," people who look more like sinners than saints. But God will use them as agents of blessing in our lives.

The second assumption we can make is that God can use ordinary people like us to help build the kingdom of God. Not only does Bethlehem imply something about the kind of ministry we will receive from others; it also says something about the kind of ministry we can give.

If God used only right-handed power, we might not be likely candidates for kingdom work. After all, most of us are not rich, influential, talented, beautiful, or intelligent enough to have much clout. But if God can use ordinary, fallible human beings to do kingdom work, we might in fact be useful. If God's power is the Bethlehem, left-handed variety, it opens the door to common folks like us. Next Sunday, we will turn our attention toward the shepherds in the Christmas story and see again how God calls and uses ordinary people.

## What About Me?

- *Bethlehem points to Golgotha.* While Bethlehem is a hint of God's left-handed power, Golgotha displays it clearly. At the cross, we see clearly that God chooses foolish things to shame the wise (see 1 Cor 1:18-25).

- *Bethlehem is easy to miss.* There were many cities in the first-century world more glamorous and influential than little Bethlehem—Rome, Alexandria, or even Jerusalem, to name a few. But Bethlehem was to be the birthplace of the king. Let's not miss God's will by looking only for glamour and glitz.

- *Bethlehem is an invitation to serve.* Because God uses places like Bethlehem and people like Joseph and Mary, our little town and our lives should be at God's disposal, too. Rather than assuming we have nothing to contribute, through Bethlehem we remember that |God sees great potential everywhere. No life is insignificant when it is placed at God's disposal.

- *Bethlehem is a place of peace.* The Bethlehem candle in the Advent wreath is also called the peace candle. At Bethlehem, we learn not only that the long-awaited king has come, but that he can use ordinary people like us. Our lives can have peace and purpose because God uses Abraham, Isaac, and Jacob.

## Resources

James Limburg, *Hosea–Micah*, Interpretation (Louisville: John Knox, 1988).

Richard B. Vinson, *Luke*, Smyth & Helwys Bible Commentary (Macon GA: Smyth & Helwys, 2008).

# O LITTLE TOWN OF BETHLEHEM

*Micah 5:2-5a; Luke 2:1-7*

## Introduction

I'll show my age. I grew up in the day of Training Union. As a child in church, the highlights of my year were the charitably termed "Better Speaker's Tournament" and "Sword Drill."

I usually entered the speaker's tournament. I won our church's tournament because I was the only entrant. As far as I can remember, I never moved beyond the associational level. Obviously, the judges were not as astute as they should have been and didn't recognize talent when it was staring at them through a pimply face.

The sword drill frightened me. Somebody called out a verse or passage in the Bible, and the first person to locate the reference stepped forward. If the people who designed the sword drill had stayed with the Gospels, Romans, Philippians, Revelation, or even Genesis and Psalms in the Hebrew Bible, I would have done well. Documents like Micah seemed like a foreign land, though, and I had trouble locating them, much less exploring them.

However, today's Old Testament reading is from Micah. This part of the book is familiar especially to people who want to "prove" that Jesus is the Messiah. "There it is," they exclaim. And of course, these people are right in one sense. There is Bethlehem, sitting smack in the heart of Micah. According to Luke, our Lord was born in that place.

## The Gospel According to Micah

Like all Bible books, Micah deserves to be heard for its own message without importing a ready-made theological grid to understand it. Micah prophesied in Judah during the second half of the eighth century BC. As James Limburg notes, this prophet possesses wonderful rhetorical skills, making abundant use of similes and metaphors. For example, Micah says in 1:4 that when the Lord comes, "the mountains will melt like wax or flow like water" (*Hosea–Micah*, Interpretation [Atlanta: John Knox, 1988] 163).

Limburg also calls attention to the sensitive spirit of this prophet. When Micah utters the message of God's judgment (1:8), he does so with a sense of personal grief (163).

In fact, Micah structures his message in alternating words of Yahweh's judgment and a message of hope. Micah calls the nation of Judah to think deeply about the need for justice, peace, and the anticipation of the coming Messiah from God.

When President Jimmy Carter was inaugurated in 1977, he had the Bible on which he took the oath of office opened to Micah. The new president then repeated the words of Micah 6:8: "He hath showed thee, O man, what is good; and what doth the LORD require of thee, but to do justly, and to love mercy, and to walk humbly with thy God" (KJV).

Understanding the focus of Micah's prophecy helps us interpret his statement about the town of Bethlehem. Micah recognizes that if the people of Judah only look at their present circumstances, they will be overwhelmed with discouragement. Because Micah is an authentic voice from God, he wants the people of Judah to understand the consequences of their distrust of Yahweh. At the same time, Micah wants the people to maintain expectancy because God is calling them to a future of hope and is shaping the "not yet."

The people of God hoped Yahweh would give them a king like David. Unfortunately, monarch after monarch disappointed the people, but prophetic hope called listeners to believe that one day, in Bethlehem—the same town in which David had been born—the Messianic King would come.

How rich this makes the book of Micah! The hope he shares is built on his faith that Yahweh works in a consistent pattern. We all face trials, temptations, discouragement, and disillusionment. We disappoint ourselves and others, and, in turn, we are disappointed. If that is the horizon of our lives, we will live with quiet despair and the taste of ashes in our mouths.

Can we have faith that there is more to life than what we see? When my children were young, we lived in Florida, not far from the ocean. Sometimes, we would pack sandwiches and drinks and go to the beach for a picnic. Late one afternoon, I stood at the edge of the ocean with David and Laura Beth on either side. "Daddy," one of them asked, "is that all there is to the world?" My child was looking at the horizon, that place where the ocean and the sky seem to join. "No," I replied. "That's all we can see with our eyes, but there's far more to our world."

Micah saw the way God worked, and so he could say, "But you, O Bethlehem of Ephrathah, who are one of the little clans of Judah, from you shall come forth for me one who is to rule in Israel" (5:2). Later, the church of Jesus the Christ would look back to say, "This is the good news that God takes the unlikely to do the unexpected."

## The Gospel According to Luke

No passage in any of the four Gospels is read more during Advent and Christmas than Luke 2:1-20. Luke 2:1-7 tells about the trip of Joseph and his expectant wife, Mary, to Joseph's home-town of Bethlehem. According to Luke's Gospel, they traveled to Bethlehem, the city of David, because of a Roman census—which was a euphemism for taxation.

The literary purpose of Luke's birth narrative is to set the coming of Jesus onto the world's stage. As Luke states, Augustus was emperor, Quirinius was governor of Syria, and in that moment of human history, Jesus was born in a stable in the back-water town of Bethlehem.

Some New Testament scholars have questioned the historical accuracy of Luke's account. For instance, Edward Schweizer points out, among other facts, that Quirinius was not governor of Syria between 9–4 bc when Herod died. Quirinius is mentioned in the story because Syria was the Roman province that encompassed both Judea and Galilee (*The Good News According to Luke*, tr. David E. Green [Atlanta: John Knox, 1984] 48). Other scholars respectfully disagree. Some point out that the

Greek word Luke uses for "governor" might be understood in a more general sense, and that there is evidence that Publius Sulpicius Quirinius may have been active in the government of Syria much earlier than his accepted dates of ad 6–12, perhaps as a special representative of the emperor: a procurator or legate.

Others suggest a far simpler explanation by noting that it is possible to translate Luke's word for "first" (*prote*) as "before" or even "former" (as in Acts 1:1). Nigel Turner suggests that a better translation of Luke 2:2 would be, "This census was before the census taken when Quirinius was governor" (*Grammatical Insights into the New Testament* [London: T. & T. Clark, 1978] 23–24). If this reading is adopted, it makes any attempt to locate Quirinius in Syria at the birth of Jesus irrelevant. Luke's point was to differentiate this prior census from one perhaps more familiar to his readers.

Still, the interpretation of this chronological footnote is subject to debate, and many prefer the more face-value reading even though it may raise theological questions. In a statement hardly designed to endear him to those who believe in the absolute historical veracity of the Bible, Schweizer states, "Probably Luke made a mistake, such as we would be apt to make about events almost a century in the past" (48).

If this were the extent of Schweizer's comments, some people would be apt to dismiss him as just another German scholar whose historical-critical method is designed to undermine our faith in the historicity of the Bible. However, those who have heard Schweizer preach know that when he proclaims the gospel, he is eloquent in his call for people to know Jesus as the Christ.

While Schweizer acknowledges that Luke may have made a "mistake" in the dating, he contends, "the question [of historical accuracy] is totally irrelevant since Luke's purpose is not to cast light on the history of taxation in Palestine but to show God speaks in an earthly historical event" (48). Schweizer further calls us to see that "There are no angels, no signs of glory, only Roman officials and more or less unhappy taxpayers—but God is nonetheless the agent of an earthshaking event" (48).

For Schweizer and for us, what happened in Bethlehem is indeed an "earthshaking event." When we sing the marvelous song of Phillips Brooks, "O Little Town of Bethlehem," we are singing about God as the agent who breaks into history not in the centers of human power, but in a place where the power of the Holy One overshadows everything and everybody, and the foundations of our worlds are shaken.

As a professor, I love the chance to be interim pastor of different churches. Some are named after communities, like Bon Air Baptist Church in Richmond, Virginia. A few times, I've been the interim of a first Baptist church such as First Baptist Church, Nashville, Tennessee. Last Advent and Christmas, I was the interim minister of Bethlehem Baptist Church in Kings Mountain, North Carolina. For the first time in my ministry, I spent Christmas at Bethlehem.

In Hebrew, the word "Bethlehem" means "house of bread." Beyond the meaning of the word, however, there was something special to me about "Christmas at Bethlehem." Maybe I'm getting sentimental as I get older. The church wasn't large in terms of membership. The buildings didn't sit at the juncture of a major intersection. The first time I went to preach a trial sermon, I took the wrong road and barely made it to Bethlehem on time. Fortunately, there was room in the pulpit that morning, even if I was almost late.

Each Sunday that I preached at Bethlehem Baptist Church, I couldn't help wondering if most people knew or even cared about what the 150–200 individuals did when we gathered in that sanctuary.

Compared to the first Bethlehem, we were big. Sometimes, cell phones rang, babies cried, and parishioners closed their eyes during the sermon and rested their chins on their chests. On some Sundays, we had a parade of people who suddenly had to go to the bathrooms. Of course, the bathrooms were on either side of the pulpit area, so the eyes of the congregation would shift to the left or the right depending on whether someone was headed to the men's room or women's room.

We didn't have any live animals in the church house, but perhaps that would have been all right. The fact is that God works in strange ways, in strange places, with some of us who probably seem strange ourselves. But that's the beauty of it.

That's the way we are reminded that it's not about us and our grandiose plans. It's about God who shook the world's foundations in—of all places—Bethlehem.

# Notes

# Notes

# WHILE SHEPHERDS WATCHED THEIR FLOCKS

*Luke 2:8-20*

## Central Question

When have I felt unworthy of God's love?

## Scripture

**Luke 2:8-20**  8  In that region there were shepherds living in the fields, keeping watch over their flock by night.  9  Then an angel of the Lord stood before them, and the glory of the Lord shone around them, and they were terrified.  10  But the angel said to them, "Do not be afraid; for see—I am bringing you good news of great joy for all the people:  11  to you is born this day in the city of David a Savior, who is the Messiah, the Lord.  12  This will be a sign for you: you will find a child wrapped in bands of cloth and lying in a manger."  13  And suddenly there was with the angel a multitude of the heavenly host, praising God and saying,  14  "Glory to God in the highest heaven, and on earth peace among those whom he favors!"  15  When the angels had left them and gone into heaven, the shepherds said to one another, "Let us go now to Bethlehem and see this thing that has taken place, which the Lord has made known to us."  16  So they went with haste and found Mary and Joseph, and the child lying in the manger.  17  When they saw this, they made known what had been told them about this child;  18  and all who heard it were amazed at what the shepherds told them.  19  But Mary treasured all these words and pondered them in her heart.  20  The shepherds returned, glorifying and praising God for all they had heard and seen, as it had been told them.

## Reflecting

In the 1970s, Thomas Harris wrote a bestselling book titled *I'm OK, You're OK*. The book presents his theory of human behavior known as "transactional analysis." Harris said that in relationships, the ideal stance is one that declares, "I'm OK, you're OK." However, he also said that is not the most prevalent relational stance. Instead, he claimed the most prevalent one is "I'm not OK, you're OK." In essence, Harris believed that most people come to relationships with a feeling of inferiority.

Whether or not we agree with Harris's theory, his premise is worth considering. Is it possible that most of us feel inferior and unworthy? Is it possible that we enter relationships with the unspoken feeling that others are "OK" but we're not? If so, how does that stance affect our relationship with God? Do we feel unworthy before God and assume that God can't use someone like us, who's "not OK"?

We continue our study today of Luke's account of Jesus' birth. Last Sunday, we focused on Bethlehem and the implications of God choosing a little village as the birthplace of the Messiah. Today we shift our focus to the shepherds in Luke's story. They were ordinary, even unworthy men, but God chose them to hear the news of the Messiah's birth before anyone else. As we consider those shepherds, we will remember again God's strange ways and God's willingness to use "the unworthy" in the work of the kingdom.

## Studying

Luke makes the shepherds central characters in his story of the birth of Jesus. The shepherds are the first to get the "good news of great joy" from the angels (v. 10). The shepherds are the first to travel to Bethlehem to verify that the Messiah is born. And the shepherds are the first to tell others about the newborn king and, therefore, become the first Christian evangelists. Fred Craddock writes,

> The shepherds belong in the story not only because they serve to tie Jesus to the shepherd king, David (2 Sam. 7:8), but also because they belong on Luke's guest list for the kingdom of God: the poor, the maimed, the blind, the lame (14:13, 21). And so the shepherds go to the city of David. The shepherds and the scene are described with some of Luke's favorite words, words he has used before: wondering, pondering in the heart, making known the revelation, praising and glorifying God. The stable is bare, but the glory of God floods the story. (36)

Rich biblical imagery surrounds shepherds. As Craddock notes, David was a shepherd who became a king. Much later, Ezekiel complained that David's descendants were false shepherds who afflicted Israel (Ezek 34), and that one day they would be punished and replaced when God himself came to be their shepherd: "I myself will search for my sheep, and will seek them out" (Ezek 34:11).

While the ideal perception of a shepherd symbolized wise leadership by God or God's representatives, the reality of the shepherds' lives did not match the lofty Old Testament metaphors. "Real" shepherds were unskilled laborers, peasants at the other end of the power scale from kings and emperors. That God would choose plain, uneducated shepherds to receive,

In Luke 15.2, we are told that Jesus received...publicans and 'sinners' and ate with them. The term 'sinners' means: (1) People who led an immoral life (e.g. adulterers, swindlers, Luke 18.11) and (2) people who followed a dishonourable calling (i.e. an occupation which notoriously involved immorality or dishonesty), and who were on that account deprived of civil rights, such as holding office, or bearing witness in legal proceedings. for example, excise-men, tax-collectors, shepherds, donkey-drivers, pedlars, and tanners. When the Pharisees and scribes asked why Jesus accepted such people as table companions, they were not expressing surprise but disapproval; they were implying that he was an irreligious man, and warning his followers not to associate with him. (Jeremias, 132) verify, and share the good news of Jesus' birth is amazing. In the first-century world, shepherds were not high on the list of "most admired people":

> It is a wonderful thing that the story should tell that the first announcement of God should come to the shepherds. The shepherds were despised by the orthodox good people of the day. Shepherds were quite unable to keep the details of the ceremonial law; they could not observe all the meticulous hand-washings and rules and regulations. Their flocks made far too constant demands on them; and so the orthodox looked down on them as very common people. It was to simple men of the fields that God's message first came. (Barclay, 17)

God chose these common shepherds to hear the good news of great joy. Once again, we see God's inclination to choose ordinary, "unworthy" people. God also showed that even these common shepherds could understand and celebrate the good news of great joy.

> But we have this treasure in clay jars, so that it may be made clear that this extraordinary power belongs to God and does not come from us. (2 Cor 4:7)

In the midst of our studies on Jesus' birth this Advent season, it's wise to pause here and remember that our gospel really is "good news of great joy." Sometimes we forget that. Sinister "isms" can creep into our lives and turn our good news into bad news.

For example, *secularism* makes us fear that all of our hopes in God are merely wistful dreams of desperate people. There's not much good news in a world with no God.

*Institutionalism* drowns our Christianity in buildings, budgets, and bylaws and makes us forget grace. There's not much good news in the church's administrative mechanisms.

Finally, *legalism* turns the good news into a rigid code of rules and regulations. There's not much good news in "oughts" and "shoulds."

Those three "isms" loom large in our culture and threaten to put a damper on our joy.

One of the blessings we may receive as we celebrate Jesus' birth is remembering the angel's song and returning to the wonder of the gospel. In Jesus, we are forgiven and set free. We received life abundant and life eternal. God is *for* us, so who or what can possibly be against us? No matter how loudly secularism, institutionalism, and legalism shout, they simply cannot overpower the sweet melody of the angelic chorus. We have good news of great joy, and we dare not forget it.

## Understanding

I'm thinking of several people who need to hear that God loves those who find themselves on the margins of society:

• The teenage girl who has posters of glamorous movie stars on her bedroom walls, but when she looks at herself in the mirror, she is disgusted at what she sees. She is too heavy, her ears are too large, and her complexion is blemished. She feels like an ugly failure.

• The writer who dreams of producing a bestseller and toils daily at her novel, but time after time, she receives terse rejection slips from publishers. She wonders if she'll ever get a book published.

• The man whose dream of a fairy-tale marriage and perfect family went down in a flaming heap of divorce and estrangement. Now he's trying to put the pieces back together—and not doing a good job of it.

• The pastor who finds himself approaching retirement age and stuck in a dying church out in the middle of nowhere. He wonders what went wrong with his ministry and why God would assign him such a pitiful place of service.

Obviously, that list could go on indefinitely. I imagine you might add others, or perhaps you might add yourself. Most of us currently live out some kind of "Plan B." We've failed at our first plan. We've been disappointed. Life has knocked us around. We've sinned and fallen far short of the

**What makes you feel unworthy to do God's work?**

glory of God. In essence, we're like the shepherds, lacking a pedigree and wishing our résumé looked better.

But God likes shepherds! To that less-than-beautiful teenage girl, that rejected and dejected writer, that disillusioned divorcé, and that downtrodden pastor, God brings good news of great joy. A big part of that good news is simply that it comes to people like them. Like those surprised shepherds in the fields, these marginalized individuals get to rejoice and find out for themselves that Jesus is real.

## What About Me?

• *Many—perhaps most—people suffer from "shepherd syndrome."* They see themselves as "not OK," and they need encouragement and affirmation from gentle, confident Christians.

• *Advent is a time to celebrate the character of God.* God chose Bethlehem as the birthplace of the king and shepherds as the first to hear the good news of great joy. God uses seemingly weak things and people to accomplish divine goals.

• *God can bless our "Plan B."* Nearly everyone has to settle for what is less than perfect, but God uses flawed, unworthy people and blesses them in spite of their imperfections.

• *The good news is really good.* Be sure you hear the angels sing this Advent season. Don't let secularism, institutionalism, legalism, or anything else drown their music.

### Resources

William Barclay, *Luke*, The Daily Study Bible (Philadelphia: Westminster, 1953).

Fred Craddock, *Luke*, Interpretation (Louisville: John Knox, 1990).

Thomas A. Harris, *I'm OK, You're OK* (New York: Avon, 1973).

Joachim Jeremias, *The Parables of Jesus*, 2nd rev. ed., trans. S. H. Hooke (New York: Charles Scribner's Sons, 1972).

Richard B. Vinson, *Luke*, Smyth & Helwys Bible Commentary (Macon GA: Smyth & Helwys, 2008).

# WHILE SHEPHERDS WATCHED THEIR FLOCKS

*Luke 2:8-20*

## Introduction

On this Sunday of Advent, the church lights the third candle in the Advent wreath. We light the candles to help us remember people from the first Christmas and also to express our hope that the fruit of the Spirit like peace and joy will become a greater part of our lives.

The shepherds represented a segment of the biblical population that was most unlikely to be invited to a celebration. Dirty, smelly, doing low-level work—these were not the types of folks who attended the grand parties of the day. Yet, here they are, front and center in Luke's account of the birth of Jesus.

The presence of the shepherds reminds us again that God works through unlikely instruments. The shepherds are called from their fields and flock to see the sign of God, a baby wrapped in cloth and lying in a manger. Later, the shepherds return to where they started, but now they are praising and glorifying God.

## While Shepherds Watched...

Most of us prepare for the celebration of Christmas. We put up the tree, hang the ornaments, wrap the gifts, and display a crèche to remind us that with all of the busyness, Jesus is the "reason for the season."

At the first Christmas, the shepherds had no way of preparing for what they were about to experience. As far as they were concerned, this was just another ordinary night. They were doing what they probably did every night and day of their lives. They stood in the fields watching their flock, not watching for the invasion of the Divine.

Into this ordinary time, the angel of the Lord appeared, the glory of the Lord shone around them, and the shepherds were terrified. Wouldn't you be terrified? I would! The shepherds were unprepared for God's coming. The glory of the Holy One showed up unannounced and unexpected. In the middle of ordinary time, the angel appeared, and suddenly it was extraordinary time. Just as it did the shepherds, this can terrify us today. God works miracles in our lives when we are simply going about our business!

Who are the shepherds, and why does Luke feature them so significantly in Jesus' birth narrative? Robert Tannehill states, "The shepherds fit the setting of Jesus' birth" (*Luke* [Nashville: Abingdon, 1996] 65). They are ordinary people who work with animals. At the same time, the echo of King David is heard when shepherds are mentioned. As Richard Vinson notes,

> "Shepherd" is rich with nuances: David was a shepherd who became a king, so the new baby born in David's city should rightly be acclaimed first to and then by shepherds. Ezekiel prophesied against false shepherds of the flock of Israel, warning that when the true shepherd came, he would protect the flock and punish the false shepherds who harmed it. (*Luke*, Smyth & Helwys Bible Commentary [Macon GA: Smyth & Helwys, 2008] 61)

Tannehill concludes, "The figure of the shepherd has the same ambiguous quality as a royal baby in a manger. A shepherd is an ordinary fellow who would not feel out of place in a stable. A shepherd is also a symbol of kingship" (65).

"In that region there were shepherds living in the fields, keeping watch over their flock by night," Luke says. Nobody made plans for God's coming. But how often have we seen that God's plans don't fit our plans? God is the God of mystery and surprise.

## But the Angel Said to Them…

The angel said several things. First, to the terrified shepherds, the message was, "Do not be afraid." But there was more. Why shouldn't they be afraid? After all, they were minding their own business, and suddenly "the glory of the Lord shone around them" (v. 9). (The Greek word for glory is *doxa*, which connotes the splendor of God.)

"For see," the angel continues, "I am bringing you good news of great joy for all the people" (v. 10). Alan Culpepper reminds us, "The familiarity of these words should not prevent us from overhearing that, first and foremost, the birth of Jesus was a sign of God's abundant grace" ("Luke," *The New Interpreter's Bible*, vol. 9 [Nashville: Abingdon, 1995] 65).

The words "good news" are a translation of the old English term, "gospel." This is a repetitive theme in Luke. God announces good news, and, as Culpepper says, "Joy and celebration are the only appropriate responses" (65).

While the Gospel of Luke is generally considered to be the most inclusive of the Gospels, the phrase "all people" actually means all the people of God, i.e., "Israel."

The response to God's coming is joy and celebration, but the angel isn't finished. "To you is born this day in the city of David a Savior, who is the Messiah, Lord. This will be a sign for you; you will find a child wrapped in bands of cloth and lying in a manger" (vv. 11-12).

Titles are significant. How does the angel designate Jesus? He is "a Savior, who is the Messiah, Lord." I have a wonderful African-American student who is completing his Doctor of Ministry degree. In his faith tradition, people in authority are referred to as "elder."

The first time I received a paper from him, I was called "Elder Bugg." I have been called lots of things in my ministry, some of which I don't know and probably don't want to know. However, I like "Elder Bugg." I told my student to keep the honorific on all his papers. Between you and me, I'm going to be disappointed when he graduates. I'll have to live on the memory that once in time I was known as "Elder."

Obviously, the names we give to Jesus are far more significant. These names reveal how we see him. The angel says to the shepherd that the one God has sent will be known as Savior and as Lord Messiah. Jesus has come to save his people from their sins. He is Savior. But Jesus is also Lord Messiah.

As Luke Timothy Johnson notes, this is a different rendering of two Greek words that are commonly applied to Jesus. The words are *christos*, which means "Anointed" and is often translated "Messiah," and *kyrios*, the Greek word for "Lord." Most of the time, we see these as two distinct titles. For example, following his resurrection, Jesus is called "Lord" and "Messiah" in Acts 2:36.

However, in Luke's Gospel, neither *christos* nor *kyrios* has a definite article preceding it. Therefore, "Lord" functions more as an adjective, and the better translation is "Lord Messiah" or "Master Messiah" (Luke Timothy Johnson, *The Gospel of Luke*, Sacra Pagina, vol. 3, ed. Daniel J. Harrington [Collegeville MN: The Liturgical Press, 1991] 50). At this point in Luke's Gospel, the angel is speaking to Jewish shepherds who would have understood that their longing for a Messiah was fulfilled in Bethlehem.

When you arrive in Bethlehem, the angel continued, "This will be a sign for you; you will find a child wrapped in bands of cloth, and lying in a manger" (2:12). The shepherds will distinguish Jesus from any other infant in Bethlehem because he will be the one in the feed trough (Vinson, 62). As Alan Culpepper notes, "The sign this time is no more than the humble surroundings of the birth that were described in the previous verses: a child wrapped in cloth bands lying in a manger" (65).

Luke is a brilliant literary artist as he paints a word picture of the coming of Christ into human history. In one moment, you and I are on a Palestinian hillside with shepherds, almost blinded by the inbreaking *doxa* of the Divine. In the next sequence of the story, we are called with the shepherds to Bethlehem where the sign is a baby lying in the manger.

Unfortunately, we have seen so many artistic renderings of the holy family at the birth of Jesus that they color the way Luke portrays the simplicity of the sign. Most of us have seen pictures of Mary with a glow around her head while she looks at a baby that appears more like a six-month-old than a newborn. The child also emits a glow. Of course, the artists are trying to communicate the divinity of Jesus.

The trouble is that's not the way Luke portrays the birth. Nothing distinguishes the birth of Jesus as different from any other birth except that it happens in Bethlehem. Like most signs, this sign from God needs the eyes of faith to interpret what God is doing.

## The Shepherds Said to One Another

When the angels appeared with good news of great joy, the shepherds decided they must go to Bethlehem to see what God was doing. Christmas is about experiencing God for ourselves. For the shepherds, it wasn't enough to hear the story. They went to see the story for themselves.

Notice Luke pays no attention to practical matters such as who watched the sheep when the shepherds left. Early in my ministry, I preached a sermon in which I suggested some fellow shepherds probably came to help watch the flock. God has to forgive a lot of bad preaching, and that was in the category of "bad preaching."

That "excursus" on my part reflected my own "angst" about turning off the lights, locking all the doors, and asking my neighbor to watch the house before I leave home to follow Jesus. Luke is about reckless faith and daring discipleship.

The shepherds went to see, but then they returned, "glorifying and praising God for all they had heard and seen" (v. 20). "Contrary to our usual tableaux," Vinson writes,

> the shepherds do not linger over the manger; they come in haste, and then leave to go spread the news. Like Mary, they seem more than a little unlikely to have been chosen to be first recipients and then bearers of God's good news, but they take to their job with enthusiasm. (62)

What changed for the shepherds was not a shift in their vocations, but it was a shift in their attitudes. The Lukan theme of celebration and joy continues.

The shepherds experienced God at work. The question then becomes, "What did that experience do to change them?" That is our question as well. Despite all the preparation we make to celebrate Christmas, the real issue is you and me. To experience the child of Bethlehem is to be born into a new kind of joy.

# Notes

# Notes

# Angels, from the Realms of Glory

*Luke 1:26-38*

## Central Question

What hard thing is God calling me to do?

## Scripture

**Luke 1:26-38**  26  In the sixth month the angel Gabriel was sent by God to a town in Galilee called Nazareth,  27  to a virgin engaged to a man whose name was Joseph, of the house of David. The virgin's name was Mary.  28  And he came to her and said, "Greetings, favored one! The Lord is with you."  29  But she was much perplexed by his words and pondered what sort of greeting this might be.  30  The angel said to her, "Do not be afraid, Mary, for you have found favor with God.  31  And now, you will conceive in your womb and bear a son, and you will name him Jesus.  32  He will be great, and will be called the Son of the Most High, and the Lord God will give to him the throne of his ancestor David.  33  He will reign over the house of Jacob forever, and of his kingdom there will be no end."  34  Mary said to the angel, "How can this be, since I am a virgin?"  35  The angel said to her, "The Holy Spirit will come upon you, and the power of the Most High will overshadow you; therefore the child to be born will be holy; he will be called Son of God.  36  And now, your relative Elizabeth in her old age has also conceived a son; and this is the sixth month for her who was said to be barren.  37  For nothing will be impossible with God."  38  Then Mary said, "Here am I, the servant of the Lord; let it be with me according to your word." Then the angel departed from her.

*Annunciation*, c. 1437–1446, Fra Angelico (1387–1455)

## Reflecting

The images we see of the holy family at the manger are often peaceful and serene. Mary and Joseph beam at the Christ child. Angels sing songs of joy. Humble shepherds gather in the barnyard to catch a glimpse of the newborn king, and mysterious wise men bring expensive gifts from the East. Over the centuries, many artists have depicted the Nativity in this way—beautiful, clean, illuminated, and calm.

When we actually read the details of the biblical story, however, we get a different picture. There's Mary, the one chosen by God and favored of God, who was both amazed and terrified at what befell her. God handpicked her, of all people, to be the mother of the Messiah. The angel Gabriel addressed her, of all people, with the announcement of God's plan. She must have felt surprised, excited...and agonized.

We typically miss the agonizing part when we read the story, but think about it for a moment. Mary was pregnant out of wedlock. She had to make a long journey from Nazareth to

Bethlehem during the last month of her pregnancy. She gave birth in a strange place with no family to support her, and perhaps not even a midwife. Her delivery room was a stable. Practically as soon as her baby boy was born, Matthew tells us, there was a death sentence on his head and the family had to flee to Egypt (Mt 2:16-21). That whole experience must have been a nightmare for Mary.

Follow the story through the Gospels and you realize her agony was just beginning. At the age of twelve, Jesus got lost in the temple and worried her sick (Lk 2:41-51). As he grew into manhood, the respectable people of the day despised and rejected him. Then, when he was just a young man, he was crucified on a cruel Roman cross between two thieves as Mary stood at the foot of that cross and wept (Jn 19:25).

Is this what it means to be favored of God? Is this what you receive when you say "yes" to God's call?

## Studying

Mary's call is one of the beloved and familiar stories in the Gospels. The call itself is full of miracles and wonders, and her response is a model of how all believers should respond to God. We look at this story today as we think about the hard things God might call us to do in the days ahead. Perhaps the simplest way to approach this passage is to consider the invitation and then the response.

*The Invitation.* The angel Gabriel extends the invitation. Three times in the first two chapters of his Gospel, Luke makes angels an integral part of his story. An angel appears to old Zechariah to inform him that he and his wife, Elizabeth, will have a son, even in their old age. Then, several months later, the same angel makes his announcement to Mary. Finally, in chapter 2, an angel appears to the shepherds declaring good news of great joy. The scene concludes with an entire choir of angels singing "glory to God in the highest heaven" (Lk 2:14).

Luke's Christmas story brims with angels! This fact can present problems, however, for many of us in the modern age who have never seen or heard an angel. Shall we merely write off these angelic appearances as part of the superstitious religion of ancient people? I think not. Perhaps the birth of Jesus demanded something outside the realm of ordinary human experience. Perhaps the coming of the long-awaited king deserved special, miraculous notice. And perhaps it is not wise to say something can't happen just because it hasn't happened *to us*.

Gabriel came to Mary, "a virgin engaged to a man whose name was Joseph, of the house of David" (1:27). Joseph and Mary's relationship at the time was similar in some ways to what we know as an engagement. In fact, it was a more solemn arrangement than our word "engaged" implies. In first-century Jewish culture, betrothal lasted for a year and was considered as binding as marriage. Only divorce could dissolve it. If a man died, the woman to whom he was betrothed was considered a widow. Once a couple was betrothed, only death could break the bond between them.

So there they were: an unlikely pair to be parents of a king. Mary was young, confused, betrothed, and willing to do whatever God demanded. Joseph was probably older, confused, betrothed, and the one who connected Jesus to the throne of David. These two unsuspecting people were in for a wild ride.

Thankfully, Gabriel's invitation also included a word of promise. Although the angel's words in 1:35 are directed exclusively to Mary as an explanation of how the birth of the Messiah would come about, we may

> One early tradition, recorded in the second-century *Protevangelium of James*, is that Joseph was a widower and that Mary was thus his second wife. This implies that he was at least a few years older than Mary, and in fact the tradition goes on to say that Joseph was well advanced in years. Of course, the Bible is silent about the couple's relative ages.

perhaps understand the promise as applying to both Mary and Joseph in a broader sense. The power of the Most High would overshadow these two, and the Holy Spirit of God would rest upon them and give them strength. Though the journey would be difficult, an unseen Companion would give them power along the way.

As a sign that these things would come to pass, Gabriel told Mary that her older relative, Elizabeth, was six months pregnant with a baby boy. That people as old as Zechariah and Elizabeth could become parents was a miracle in itself, but all of this, Gabriel said, was from God. To drive home his point, the angel said what another angel said centuries earlier to Abraham and Sarah when they doubted their ability to have a child: "For nothing will be impossible with God" (1:37; see Gen 18:14).

*The Response.* Mary's response to God's invitation was both simple and profound: "Here am I, the servant of the Lord; let it be with me according to your word" (1:38). Luke 1:46-55 offers an addendum to that response in the form of Mary's *Magnificat*. It is a hymn of praise to God for choosing her to be the mother of the Messiah and of gratitude for God's willingness to use unlikely people and places.

When Gabriel departs from Mary, the transaction is complete. God gave the invitation, and Mary responded. God said, "Mary, will you help me?" Mary answered with an exuberant "yes."

There are four songs in Luke's Christmas story:

- Mary's Song (1:46-55)
- Zechariah's Song (1:67-69)
- The Angels' Song (2:13-14)
- Simeon's Song (2:29-32)

She scarcely knew what she was getting into, but her answer to God serves as an eternal example of genuine faith. In effect, young, overwhelmed, wide-eyed Mary said, "I don't understand what this involves, God, but I'm ready to go."

## Understanding

Some older hymnals contain the song "Here Is My Life." The chorus to the song goes,

> Here is my life, I want to live it. Here is my life, I want to give it.
> Serving my fellow man, doing the will of God,
> Here is my life, here is my life, here is my life.
> (Seabough and Bartlett, 356)

I thought of this song as I studied our passage because that's what Mary said. God knocked on her door, asking her to take a risk and begin a dangerous adventure. Essentially, Mary said, "Here is my life."

As we know from following her story through the Gospels, that decision made her vulnerable to pain and disappointment. God asked Mary to do a terribly difficult thing. When we read her story, we see clearly that receiving and responding to a call from God can lead to both servanthood and suffering.

In every generation, someone asserts that the real people of God have it easy. During a recent visit to the bookstore, I saw a book titled *God Wants You Rich*. There are probably books out there with titles like *God Wants You Happy*, *God Wants You Carefree*, and *God Wants You Successful*, too. My guess is that, were she alive today, Mary wouldn't buy those books. Nor would Joseph or Jesus. They all knew better. God wants us *faithful*.

> **?** What details of Mary's life serve as an example for Christian discipleship? What qualities of Mary do you wish were more evident in your life?

I have frequently prayed that God would come out in the open and give me an obvious revelation. In essence, I've always wanted an angel to appear to me. After remembering Mary's experience, I realize I didn't know what I was praying for. Mary's experience reminds me that angels show up not only to sing and surprise; they also come with calls for suffering and sacrifice.

Be careful, then, before you ask for angels. You might get more than you prayed for.

## What About Me?

- *Have you ever prayed for angels?* Mary's experience reminds us that God sends angels for better reasons than to meet our demands for certainty. God's revelation comes to those who serve *and* sacrifice.

- *What does Mary teach us about faith?* Often we think of faith as resting in the goodness of God, but faith also involves struggle, disappointment, and pain. Read Hebrews 11 if you want to get a picture of biblical faith.

- *What hard thing is God calling us to do?* Mary is not the only person God has called to do something difficult. What hard thing must we do to answer God's call?

- *Can we still sing?* Mary sang the *Magnificat* after God called her. We can only hope that, at the end of her life, after all of the pain and struggle, she was still able to sing. Faith sings even through trouble.

## Resources

Ed Seabough and Gene Bartlett, "Here Is My Life," *The Baptist Hymnal* (Nashville: Convention, 1975) 356.

# ANGELS, FROM THE REALMS OF GLORY

*Luke 1:26-38*

## Introduction

When I read the Christmas story in Luke's Gospel, I am over-whelmed by its beautiful poetry and lyrical quality. It sounds soft and gentle. An angel, Gabriel, comes as a messenger to a virgin named Mary and says, "Greetings, favored one! The Lord is with you" (1:28b).

These are moving words, but not in the soft, tender way in which I have often read about this encounter of God's messenger with Mary. Don't look now, but Mary's whole life is about to be drastically altered. This is hardly a Hallmark moment of greeting. Gabriel should have begun by saying, "Look out!"

I have two friends who felt God's call to be missionaries in Hungary. As the three of us dined at a nice restaurant, they told me about a sense of divine movement in their lives. "Why would you want to do that?" I asked. "You have a wonderful job in an outstanding church. Your daughters are in school, and you'll have to leave them. It really sounds like a crazy idea to me." Do you know what? My friends didn't listen to me. They listened to God, and every email I have received from them sounds as if they could not be more fulfilled.

Frankly, if an angel comes to me and says, "Greetings," I'm likely to head in the opposite direction. That's too bad, because every time we hear from Mary in the Gospels, she seems to be fulfilled.

## God Acts

As Alan Culpepper reminds us, "The central figure in the annunciation is neither Gabriel nor Mary—it is the gracious God of Israel" (*Luke*, The New Interpreter's Bible, vol. 9 [Nashville: Abingdon, 1995] 50–51). With all of the human figures mentioned in Luke's Gospel surrounding the birth of Jesus and with the appearance of the angel, this is really a story about the God who acts in human history.

The Gospel of Luke tells us, "In the sixth month the angel Gabriel was sent by God" (v. 26). The protagonist in the first Christmas pageant was not the messenger, Gabriel, or the mother, Mary, but rather it was the Holy One who sent the messenger and the message into the midst of human history.

Luke is artful in bringing together the earthly and the eternal. In the sixth month after Gabriel told Elizabeth that she and Zechariah would be blessed with a son, Mary discovers that she is "favored" by God. John and Jesus were cousins by birth and brothers in both the proclamation of repentance and the invitation to follow the God who sent them both.

Even with the numerous historical details and individuals who take part in this drama of the incarnation, Luke wants us never to forget that God is the one who sent Gabriel. The message Gabriel delivers is the one the Almighty composed.

John Westerhoff says, "The health of our spiritual life is also directly related to our image of God" (*Spiritual Life: The Foundation for Preaching and Teaching* [Louisville: Westminster/John Knox, 1994] 3). How do we imagine God? How do we view God? Is the God whom we worship involved in our lives? Abraham Joshua Heschel, the Jewish philosopher and theologian, once referred to Yahweh as the "most moved mover."

In some churches where I have served, I have done what I call "children's moments." I deliberately don't call it a "children's sermon" because, as Thomas Long says, that plays into the Protestant heresy that the only critical component in the worship service is the sermon.

One Sunday morning I was telling the story of Jesus' love for the children. All of a sudden, one of the children asked, "Where is God?" Frankly, that was not the subject. I wondered what to do. Tell the child to save the question for later? Confess that in seminary we didn't talk about God in language that made sense to a seven-year-old?

The congregation enjoyed watching me squirm. What should I say? Should I tell him that God is in his heart or that God is everywhere, both of which raise more questions to which I don't have the answers?

With all of my sidestepping and evasion, I have to admit that it is a good question. Where is God? The God of Luke is active, involved, and on the move in unexpected ways in the lives of people. The Gospel states, "In the sixth month the angel Gabriel was sent by God" (v. 26).

## Mary Responds

Angels may come from "realms of glory" as the title of our lesson suggests, but these angels have a way of disrupting our lives and making us wonder if we truly wish to hear from "realms of glory." Mary certainly wondered what God was doing.

This young woman was engaged to Joseph. Plans had been made, and the destiny of her life seemed set. However, the words of God through Gabriel came: "Greetings, favored one! The Lord is with you" (v. 28).

We accept most greetings at face value, but Mary knew there was more to this particular greeting. Mary was perplexed, and she pondered what this visit meant.

Then Gabriel announced God's intention. Mary would conceive a child. Being a devout Jew, Mary pointed out to the angel that she was a virgin. At this juncture, Mary assumed the father would be Joseph. Was she ever surprised! The father was the Spirit of God, and the child would be called the Son of God. After she and Gabriel discussed her cousin Elizabeth, who was expecting a child she never thought she could have in her old age, it was time for Mary's final answer to God.

Mary is perplexed. She's pondering what is transpiring in her life. Apparently, she's fearful at the appearance of the angel because the messenger's first words following the greeting are, "Do not be afraid, Mary" (v. 30).

What would be Mary's response? Afraid, perplexed, and pondering—how would she choose to answer God? In her poem "Magellan," Mary Oliver writes, "Let us risk the wildest places, lest we go down in comfort and despair" (cited in Sam M. Intrator, ed., *Living the Questions: Essays Inspired by the Work and Life of Parker J. Palmer* [San Francisco: Jossey-Bass, 2005] 233). This young Jewish woman made a choice. Her life would not be spent in "comfort and despair." In that folksy translation called *The Cotton Patch Gospel*, Clarence Jordan has Mary respond to Gabriel, "All right then, I am at the Lord's service. I want it to be just as you have said" (*Clarence Jordan's Cotton Patch Gospel: Luke and Acts* [Macon GA: Smyth & Helwys, 2004] 4).

Fred Craddock describes Mary's response by saying, "Mary bows in humble obedience to the Word of God" (*Luke*, Interpretation [Louisville: John Knox, 1990] 28). A story that begins with an "angel come from glory" concludes with an unmarried woman, perhaps even a girl no older than in her early teens, saying a brave yes to a God who calls her, as Mary Oliver says, "to the wildest places" (Intrator, 233).

As a minister who preaches almost every Sunday, I'm constantly reevaluating the time of invitation. In our free-church tradition, most of us conclude our worship services by inviting people to respond to the beckoning of God in their lives. While we invite people to do things such as join the church or recommit their lives to Jesus, our fundamental invitation is to ask people to follow the Christ.

As a minister, sometimes I have asked people to become "Christians." While Christian is a good word and means "little Christ," the noun does not capture the vital, organic, even transcendent nature of the call Jesus issues to people in the Gospels. When I invited people to become Christians, I sounded as if I were asking them to join the Rotary Club. No angels—no mediators from the realm of glory—were needed. I was asking them to join a club that frankly had fewer requirements than some civic clubs of which I've been a member.

The Gospel of Luke, with its emphasis on following Jesus and being on a journey with him, has helped me to understand better the risky nature of saying "yes" to the Divine One. At some point in her life, Mary had said "yes" to follow the God of Israel. Did she have any ideas of the other ways she would have to say "yes" to this God? Do any of us ever fully understand that when we say yes to follow Jesus on the journey of discipleship, we open ourselves to "angels from the realms of glory" who call us in ways that we can never anticipate?

For all of the light and joy that most of us bring to the Christmas season, let's not forget the risk and danger of saying "yes" to the God who calls us to a journey without roadmaps.

Once in a while, I reach for an old book of sermons. One of my favorite preachers is Harry Emerson Fosdick, longtime pastor of Riverside Church in New York City. Although some of Fosdick's language is archaic, he has a wonderful way of wrapping words around profound truths. In a lecture on preaching, Fosdick wrote,

> The one vital thing in religion is first-hand personal experience. Religion is the most intimate, incommunicable fellowship of the human soul.... You never know God at all until you know him for yourself. The only God you will ever know is the God you do know for yourself. (*Christianity and Progress* [New York: Revell, 1922] 160)

"Greetings, favored one," the angel, mediator, messenger of God said. God knew who Mary was. Mary knew who God was. That is a recipe for delight and for danger!

# Notes

# Notes

# OF THE FATHER'S LOVE
# BEGOTTEN

*John 1:1-18*

## Central Question

How is the birth of Christ relevant to my life?

## Scripture

**John 1:1-18**  1  In the beginning was the Word, and the Word was with God, and the Word was God.  2  He was in the beginning with God.  3  All things came into being through him, and without him not one thing came into being. What has come into being  4  in him was life, and the life was the light of all people.  5  The light shines in the darkness, and the darkness did not overcome it.  6  There was a man sent from God, whose name was John.  7  He came as a witness to testify to the light, so that all might believe through him.  8  He himself was not the light, but he came to testify to the light.  9  The true light, which enlightens everyone, was coming into the world.  10  He was in the world, and the world came into being through him; yet the world did not know him.  11  He came to what was his own, and his own people did not accept him.  12  But to all who received him, who believed in his name, he gave power to become children of God,  13  who were born, not of blood or of the will of the flesh or of the will of man, but of God.  14  And the Word became flesh and lived among us, and we have seen his glory, the glory as of a father's only son, full of grace and truth.  15  (John testified to him and cried out, "This was he of whom I said, 'He who comes after me ranks ahead of me because he was before me.'")  16  From his fullness we have all received, grace upon grace.  17  The law indeed was given through Moses; grace and truth came through Jesus Christ.  18  No one has ever seen God. It is God the only Son, who is close to the Father's heart, who has made him known.

## Reflecting

In the 1960s, John Steinbeck wrote a bestselling book titled *Travels with Charley*. The book chronicled Steinbeck's travels around America with his dog. It was just the two of them in a pickup truck, carefree and rootless, wandering around the country as a couple of vagabonds.

After I finished reading the book, I wanted to take a trip of my own. It seemed so inviting to pull up roots and hit the road. I could almost imagine it—no responsibilities, no committee meetings, no sermon preparation, and no day planner. Just my wife, Sherry, and me and the open road.

Frankly, there are many days when life in general looks a lot more inviting than life in particular. Life in particular gets pretty messy. Dealing with specific people, attending a specific church, working at a specific job—all of that is demanding and draining.

As we gather this week, just two days after Christmas, we take heart in the midst of our messy, particular lives because we remember that God has a preference for the particular. The birth of Jesus reminds us that God got tangled up in the specifics of human history. John says, "the Word became flesh and lived among us" (1:14).

Today we look at John's "Christmas story." Unlike the story in Luke that we've studied for the past few weeks, John has no Bethlehem, no shepherds, and no angels. He doesn't even have a Mary and a Joseph! John gives us theological poetry celebrating who Jesus was and why Jesus came.

## Studying

Only two characters play a part in John's Christmas story: Jesus and John the Baptist. The writer never even calls Jesus by name. In John's prologue, Jesus is the *logos*, the creative, dynamic word of God. Nevertheless, Jesus and John give the writer of the Fourth Gospel enough material to sketch his Christmas story.

The announcer of the birth of the King is a man named John (1:6-9; 1:19-34). He is a witness to the Messiah, but he is not the Messiah himself. Throughout the Gospel of John, John the Baptist is consistently assigned a lesser place than Jesus. Apparently so many revered him that the possibility existed of him becoming an object of worship. In the book of Acts, for example, the apostle Paul meets people in Ephesus who experienced the baptism of John but never heard of Jesus. John the Baptist was well known and highly admired, so the Gospel writer consistently puts him in his place. John was a witness to the Messiah, but the Messiah is Jesus, the living Word of God.

This Word, naturally, gets most of the Evangelist's attention in the prologue to his Gospel. The Word was with God from the beginning and participated in the creation of

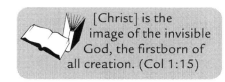

[Christ] is the image of the invisible God, the firstborn of all creation. (Col 1:15)

the world. To take it a step further, the Word *was* God, and to see and hear him was to see and hear God. The divinity of Christ is asserted more emphatically in the Fourth Gospel than practically anywhere else in Scripture. In John 14, when Philip asks Jesus to "show us the Father and we will be satisfied," Jesus responds, "Whoever has seen me has seen the Father" (Jn 14:8-9). Near the end of the Gospel, when Thomas finally sees the risen Christ, he exclaims, "My Lord and my God!" (Jn 20:28). Central to John's story of Jesus is the confession that the Word "was God" (Jn 1:2).

This living Word came into the world to bring light in the midst of darkness, and the world could not diminish his light. Sadly, the world neither recognized nor accepted him. "He came to what was his own," the Gospel writer states, "and his own people did not accept him" (1:11). When you think about it, it's easy to see why the people failed to recognize and accept Jesus. They were looking for a different kind of messiah, a warrior on a white horse, a politician wielding a gavel, someone with forceful power.

As we have seen the last few weeks, what they got was a baby born in the unlikely village of Bethlehem, visited by lowly shepherds, and birthed by a teenaged girl. None of that looked or sounded like the messiah the Jews expected. When he grew up and told simple stories to simple people

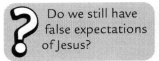

Do we still have false expectations of Jesus?

and chose fishermen and tax collectors to be his followers, their suspicions were confirmed. When he died as a common criminal on a Roman cross, they knew it for sure. No messiah would die like that.

John's assertion that "his own people did not accept him" is not surprising. Most people in that day would come to the same conclusion: This Jesus is not the long-awaited king. Surprisingly, some people did believe. Not many, to be sure, but enough to start a movement, enough for the spark of the gospel to begin to fan into flames and spread. To the few who received the Word and believed in his name, he gave power to become the children of God, to be born of God (1:12).

Those who believed became convinced that this Jesus was God in the flesh. John proclaims for all these believers: "And the Word became flesh and lived among us, and we have seen his glory, the glory as of a father's only son, full of grace and truth" (1:14). John is so convinced that this Word is God in the flesh that he repeats himself: "No one has ever seen God. It is God the only Son, who is close to the Father's heart, who has made him known" (1:18).

The first eighteen verses of John soar to majestic theological heights. In these verses, John touches on some of the most profound words and concepts in Christian theology: Word, light, life, darkness, witness, world, believe, power, glory, grace, and truth. You could write a comprehensive theological statement just using those words from John's prologue.

One of the clear truths we recognize when reading John's prologue is that God's love had to become focused and particular. The only way for God to love the world was to send his Son into the world so that everyone who believes in him should not perish but have eternal life (Jn 3:16). God could love the whole world only by sending Jesus into a particular time and place.

For God, love is particular. As we finish our study of the birth of the King, that truth is a fine finale for us. Like God's, our love must be particular, too. Like God, we can't "love in general"; we must love specific people in specific ways.

## Understanding

John's poetic prologue helps us celebrate the amazing love of God that became particular in Jesus. It also serves as a model to us as we go about the business of daily living. Love is always particular.

We might say, "Oh, I just love children," but unless we love rambunctious Anna with the runny nose and missing front tooth, we don't know what love is. Or we might say, "I love old people," but unless we love Mrs. Franklin wrapped in the blanket who spends her days in the rocking chair, we don't know what love is.

This text can help us remember the indispensability of our focused love. The baby in the crib will die without our love. The child ambling off to kindergarten cannot navigate the choppy seas of school life without our undivided attention. The surly teenager needs our touch far more than she will ever admit. The newlywed young woman still needs our concentrated care. The poor guy fighting the mid-life blues needs our love as much or more than ever. The bedridden woman in the nursing home can go on living only if we take delight in her.

In her book *Where the Wind Begins*, Paula D'Arcy writes,

> The formula for finding your own, primary mission is here: Put down this book. Walk outside your house, trailer, or apartment. Look in through a window. Now you see where Christ has sent you. Serving starts where you are. If you understand that your mission to the faces at your table, no matter how few, ranks in importance with the mission of a great evangelist to crowds of thousands, then you have begun to understand love. (36–37)

Love always becomes flesh and lives among particular people. It was true for God, and it is true for us too.

## What About Me?

- *God has always been like Jesus.* We can celebrate the character of God because we have seen how loving and gracious Jesus was.

- *The Word is Immanuel.* As we saw in the first lesson of this unit, the Messiah was going to be Immanuel, "God with us." John's prologue reaffirms that truth and reminds us that our God has "walked a mile in our shoes."

- *Love is always particular.* What specific people should we care for this week? Who needs our undivided attention and love right now?

- *If we want the job, we're hired.* No experience is necessary in the field of love. We don't have to be educated, wealthy, or talented to qualify. We simply have to know the indispensability of love and be willing to offer it to one person.

## Resource

William Barclay, *The Gospel of John*, vol. 1 (Philadelphia: Westminster, 1955).

Paula D'Arcy, *Where the Wind Begins* (Wheaton: Harold Shaw, 1984).

John Steinbeck, *Travels with Charley* (New York: Bantam, 1968).

# OF THE FATHER'S LOVE
# BEGOTTEN

*John 1:1-18*

## Introduction

When I saw that the purpose of this lesson was to try to explain
the Incarnation, I wished I had agreed to write the four previous
lessons and left this to someone else. Trying to explain how Jesus
was both divine and human has been the subject of numerous
scholarly books. When the early church wrestled with this at its
various councils, those scholars said Jesus was completely divine
and completely human. That doesn't compute to our rational
minds, but that was the conclusion. Jesus is 100% God and 100%
human.

The first eighteen verses of John's Gospel are the prologue.
While John has always been considered a Gospel, it is approached
differently than Matthew, Mark, and Luke. These first three
books of the New Testament are called Synoptic Gospels, from a
Greek word that means "seen together." John's Gospel includes
stories that are absent from the other three, such as Jesus turning
water into wine and the resuscitation of Lazarus. It also portrays
Jesus differently than the Synoptics, with several long soliloquies
and distinctive terminology. Through recounting only a handful
of Jesus' miraculous "signs," using "I am" statements (which only
appear in John), and communicating in a unique, meditative
tone, the Fourth Gospel explores what it means to claim that
Jesus is indeed the Son of God (see Jn 20:31).

Nevertheless, the Gospel of John is a Gospel. It is an attempt
to express who Jesus is and why he is significant for people's lives.
As with the other Gospels, John is not an objective biography
attempting simply to communicate biographical information

about Jesus. John's fundamental purpose is to convey to readers that Jesus is the incarnate Son of God.

## The Word in Creation (1:1-5)

D. Moody Smith divides the prologue of John into three major sections (*John*, Abingdon New Testament Commentaries [Nashville: Abingdon, 1999] 49–64). The first section is the Word in creation. Like the Old Testament book of Genesis, the Gospel of John opens with "In the beginning." As Smith notes, both John and Genesis give a narration about creation. The difference is that in the Gospel, this creation revolves around the one we call Jesus (Smith, 2).

Furthermore, Jesus, called "the Word" (*logos* in Greek) in John's prologue, was not only present in the original creation; he also now makes possible a new creation (Robert Kysar, *John's Story of Jesus* [Philadelpha: Fortress, 1984) 15).

There is widespread agreement among scholars that we should read John's prologue against the background of ancient Jewish wisdom speculation. Both the Johannine logos and the personified Wisdom of Jewish thought are understood as preexistent, "with God" (see Prov 8:3), divine, the instrument of creation, the source of life, etc. (see Charles H. Talbert, *Reading John: A Literary and Theological Commentary on the Fourth Gospel and Johannine Epistles*, rev. ed. [Macon GA: Smyth & Helwys, 2005] 71–73).

In ancient Judaism, Wisdom and the Word of God are often used interchangeably for the same reality (Talbert, 73). For example, the apocryphal book Wisdom of Solomon states,

> O God of my ancestors and Lord of mercy,
> who have made all things by your *word*,
> and by your *wisdom* have formed humankind
> to have dominion over the creatures you have made.... (9:1-2)

In parallel lines, God's agent in creation is described as either the Word of God or the Wisdom of God.

While New Testament scholars disagree on the nuances that should be attached to John's concept of the *logos*, the important point is that this preexistent, incarnate Word from God is an attempt to disclose the Divine. God is seeking to make himself known through this christological communication.

The writer of the Gospel of John wants us to know that this is a transformative Word. Through Jesus, the Word, the Holy One speaks about the possibility for us to be a new creation.

## The Word Enters History (1:6-13)

As in the Synoptic Gospels' accounts of Jesus' life and ministry, John the baptizer is a witness to testify to the "light" that is Jesus. The writer of the Gospel of John continues the image of Jesus as "light." This metaphor is used to identify the eternal, present Word of God who has come with the mission of salvation into the darkness of people's worlds. John was the precursor to this incarnation of the light. The Gospel writer wants readers to understand the importance of John as a witness but not to mistake the forerunner as the light itself.

Interestingly, some outstanding contemporary professors of preaching, such as Anna Carter Florence at Columbia Presbyterian Seminary in Decatur, Georgia, and Thomas Long at Candler School of Theology in Atlanta, have reminded preachers that their fundamental task is to give testimony or to bear witness to Jesus as the light of the world.

Effective teachers of the Bible can often inadvertently draw attention to themselves. Obviously, we are drawn to winsome teachers and preachers who teach and preach in ways that help us understand the Bible and see its connection to our lives. Apparently, John the Baptist had those qualities of communication and personality that drew people to travel from their comfort zones into the uncomfortable wilderness to hear him preach.

Yet, as capable as the messenger is, he or she is always in service to the message. In this case, the message itself is the One who is both God and sent from God to be light in our darkness.

The Fourth Gospel makes clear that the message is for everyone, but that Jesus' first audience was "his own" (v. 11). As Raymond Brown points out, "The reference is clearly to the people of Israel" (*The Gospel according to John, 1–12*, The Anchor Bible [Garden City NY: Doubleday, 1966] 10).

Sometimes these references to the priority of the people of Israel make those of us who are non-Jews feel as if we are simply an afterthought in God's invitation. However, Yahweh's connection to Israel was deep, and we would be more surprised if God's love for God's people was so easily forsaken. The fact that God cares so much for "his own" reminds us of the steadfast mercy of God so beautifully described in the Hebrew word *chesed* ("steadfast love" or "loving-kindness"). Those of us who are a part of the new covenant can be reassured that we, too, are loved with such relentless grace.

## The Word Is Seen and Received in the Community (1:14-18)

While the entire prologue of John is important to help us understand who Jesus is, the culmination of what some scholars interpret as a hymn is verse 14. There, the Gospel writer states, "And the Word became flesh and lived among us, and we have seen his glory, the glory as of a father's only son, full of grace and truth." D. Moody Smith says, "John 1:14 is often regarded as the classical statement of the Christian doctrine of the Incarnation, as 3:16 aptly states the doctrine of salvation" (Smith, 58).

We need to remember that the Christian doctrine of the Trinity does not imply three distinct deities. Interestingly, the word "Trinity" never appears in the New Testament. The idea of a Triune God was developed by the church fathers to preserve the monotheistic nature of God and at the same time explain how this one God could be revealed to the world in three persons: Father, Son, and Holy Spirit.

Strongly monotheistic faiths such as Judaism and Islam have enormous difficulties accepting the notion of "God in three persons." To a devout Jew or Muslim, the concept of Trinity appears to sabotage the foundational belief in monotheism. Indeed, the Christian apologists who first attempted to explain the Trinity found it was no easy task. At the Council of Nicea in AD 325, the church leaders chose the word "begotten" to explain how the Son came from the Father. (Later councils explained that the Holy Spirit "proceeds" from the Father.) By using the word "begotten," they attempted to preserve the unity of God and show that God could be known in the persons of the Trinity.

While the concept is difficult to explain, nevertheless, John is eager to show that Jesus is the revelation of the Father's love. God is always "other" than we are, but in Jesus, the Divine "pitched his tent with us"—a more literal translation of the Greek words usually translated "dwelt among us." God's pitching his tent with us in Jesus of Nazareth is a popular rendering of the incarnation.

While you and I may struggle intellectually with the concept of the Trinity, by faith we believe that God has fully entered the stream of human history. Jesus comes not on a divine whim but as a result of divine love. The story behind the story of Christmas is that there is a God who loves us and who comes to live with us.

Fred Craddock contends, "No higher compliment could come to the human community than that the Word had joined it, in flesh" (*John*, Knox Preaching Guides, John H. Hayes, ed. [Atlanta: John Knox, 1982] 13). What an interesting perspective on the Incarnation! God compliments us by coming to us. Despite the fact of human disobedience against the divine intention for creation, the Holy One doesn't turn against us; instead, in an incredible act of mercy, God comes to us.

As the Gospel continues to emphasize, John the Baptist gives witness to us about Jesus Christ. A part of that testimony is captured in that sublime Johannine phrase, "From his [Jesus'] fullness we have all received, grace upon grace" (v. 16).

This phrase, "grace upon grace," reinforces the lyrical quality of the Gospel of John. "Grace upon grace" has a doxological feel to it. While "fullness" is a word more common in the writings of the Apostle Paul, John uses it in this context to indicate that all of God is found in this incarnate Word God communicates to us.

Does any of this explain clearly the Incarnation? Absolutely not! As with so many other important facets of our Christian faith, we ultimately "stand amazed in the presence." What we do believe is the boundless love of God to humankind. We believe that love was most fully expressed and communicated to us in the person of Jesus Christ. If we believe in that love deeply enough, then we have heard the message, and we have experienced the coming of the Word into our own lives.

# Notes

# Notes

### 1 Peter
#### Keep Hope Alive

This study of First Peter focuses on keeping hope alive in the face of pressures and circumstances that could possibly extinguish it completely, or worse, turn authentic faith into a pale replica of the real thing.

### Apocalyptic Literature

This study examines five apocalyptic texts in the Bible—from Zechariah, Daniel, Matthew, and Revelation. With each new year bringing a new prediction of impending doom, it is always a perfect time to get the story straight. Apocalyptic literature does not address the future. It addresses our present.

### Approaching a Missional Mindset

The World isn't the same as it once was. We must be the church in a new place, in unimagined ways, and with a wider range of people. Engage your small group with the radical and refreshing challenge of developing a "missional lifestyle."

### Baptist Freedom
#### Celebrating Our Baptist Heritage

What makes a Baptist a Baptist? Of course, the ultimate answer is simple: membership in a local Baptist church. But there are all kinds of Baptist churches! What are the spiritual and theological marks of a Baptist? What is the shape and the feel of Baptist Christianity?

### The Bible and the Arts

God has used artistic expression throughout the centuries to convey truth, offer blessing, and urge believers to deeper faithfulness. In modern life, artistic expression flourishes, from movies to books to music to paintings to photographs. Sometimes artists are intentional about trying to portray God's truths. Other times, perhaps God is working even when the artist is unaware of it. As believers, we may hear and see God at work in many art forms.

### Challenges of the Christian Life

The way of the cross is difficult, and taking Jesus seriously means looking honestly at how we fall short of God's best hopes for us and seeing how much we need God's grace. For all of us there are times when we need to remember that Christ is our saving grace and recommit ourselves to the journey of faith, rediscovering, again and again, the life-giving purpose described in the book of Ephesians.

### Christ Is Born!

Even in the midst of difficult circumstances, Advent is a time when we can find hope. Much like today, people in the 1st century church faced struggles. Examining the Gospel of Matthew, lessons include "Waiting for Christ," "Preparing for Christ," "Expecting Christ," "Announcing Christ," and "The Arrival of Christ."

### Christians and Hunger

These sessions challenge us to apply gospel lenses and holy imagination to what literally gives us energy to live: food. With God's grace, we have the opportunity to imagine communities where tables are large and all are fed.

### Christmas in Mark

In the early chapters of Mark, we will encounter a Christmas story. This story, however, will not be quite like the one told by other Gospel writers, but it will resonate with the reality of your life. Mark doesn't deny the beauty or reality of the nativity; however, he seems to believe that Christmas begins—the gospel begins—when Christ intrudes upon the hard realities of life.

## The Church on a Mission

What does it mean to be a church on a mission? The lesson of Acts 1:8 is that we must simultaneously carry out Christ's mandate at home, in our region, in places that have been our blind spots, and around the world.

## Colossians
### Living the Faith Faithfully

Paul's letter to the Colossians begins with a high-minded philosophical defense of the faith, but concludes with a collection of extremely practical advice for living by faith. This study addresses the questions many Christians face today, helping them apply Paul's practical advice in their own lives.

## Easter Confessions

Easter confession is often found on many different lips in the Gospel of John. When we listen carefully, those ancient confessions still echo into this new millennium.

## Embracing the Word of God

We live during a time of transition in Christian history. Basic assumptions about the truth of the Christian faith are being questioned, not only by nonbelievers, but by Christians themselves. First John offers a starting point for understanding of what it means to "be" Christian.

## Esther: A Woman of Discretion and Valor

The book of Esther is not a record of historical facts as such. Rather, it is a magnificent narrative that refuses to interpret life as being driven by coincidence or happenstance. In the otherwise unknown characters of Esther, Haman, and Mordecai, we trace the movement of the divine hand as God collaborates with God's risk-taking people to rescue them from the hand of their enemies.

## Facing Life's Challenges

This study explores four significant challenges common to most persons of faith: the challenge of new light, the challenge of time's limit, the challenge of living with mystery, and the challenge of authentic spirituality. Although these issues are neither simple nor easy to ponder, this study effectively leads us in confronting these challenges.

### Galatians
#### Freedom in Christ

Paul wrote with fiery passion, as you will notice from the opening paragraphs of this letter to the Galatians. But his language reveals that he was writing about a crucially important issue—the very nature of salvation in Christ.

### A Holy and Surprising Birth

Christmas begins here—discover these five love stories from the book of Luke and renew your appreciation of God's laborious effort to birth our salvation.

### How Does the Church Decide?

An array of decisions draw energy and time from church members. These decisions may be theological, such as mode of baptism, aesthetic, such as the color of the sanctuary carpet, or functional, such as the selection of a new minister. This study will consider how the church has made its decisions in the past to help guide our decisions today.

### Is God Calling?

Witness the varying forms of God's call, the variety of people called, and the variety of responses. Perhaps God's call to you will become clearer.

### James
#### Gaining True Wisdom

If we'll be honest with God and ourselves as we study what James says, we can make great strides toward wisdom and a living faith.

### Life Lessons from Bathsheba

Who was Bathsheba? She was a complex figure who developed from the silent object of David's lust into a powerful, vocal, and influential queen mother.

## Life Lessons from David

In the Bible, we catch David in the various stages of the human journey: childhood, adolescence, adulthood, and senior adulthood. From the biblical treatment of the stages of David's life, we can land some insights to assist us in better understanding the human journey.

## The Matriarchs

The matriarchs of Genesis offer their lives as a testimony of faith, perseverance, and audacity. We learn from their mistakes and suffering. We will gain the hope of Hagar, the joy of Sarah, and the audacity of Rebekah as we are challenged to examine our prejudices and our insecurities while studying Esau and Jacob's wives.

## Moses
### From the Burning Bush to the Promised Land

We would do well to trace the life of Moses so we might discover how his life changed, both personally and as Israel's leader, as he learned what it meant to love God with all his heart, soul, and strength.

## Old Testament Promises to God

Some individuals may feel that our promises couldn't possibly mean anything to God. Perhaps the real question is this: under what circumstances should or do we make such promises? The Old Testament contains several examples of people making promises to God, using the unique form of a biblical "vow."

## The Passion of Christ

The four lessons in this unit highlight the faith struggles of the early disciples. In lesson one, Jesus addresses the issues of faith and practice. In lesson two, we meet Judas who, like us, struggled with God's Kingdom and human kingdoms. In lesson three, the issue of temptation reminds us that our faith journey is a constant challenge. Lesson Four invites us to remember Peter's experience of "faith failure." Peter's failure, however, is not the final word. There is forgiveness.

### The Prayer Life of Jesus

The study of Jesus' prayer life can deepen our own prayer practices. These five sessions examine the importance of prayer at various stages of Jesus' life and ministry. He made no important decisions without consulting God.

### Proverbs for Living

Long ago, a collection of wise teachers committed themselves to the ways of God and collected this wisdom into what we know as the book of Proverbs. These four lessons explore the simple truth of Proverbs: there is a good life to be had—a life lived in faithfulness to God.

### Seeking Holiness in the Sermon on the Mount

The Sermon on the Mount has long been recognized as the pinnacle of Jesus' teaching. But with this importance in mind, it's easy to think of Jesus' teachings as lofty and idealistic, offering little guidance for everyday life. Perhaps Jesus' sermon allows us to see beyond ourselves, beyond our own failures and shortcomings—revealing God's intention for our lives.

### Spiritual Disciplines
#### Obligation or Opportunity?

The spiritual disciplines help deepen a believer's faith and increases his or her intimacy with Christ. In this study, we take a deeper look at some of the disciplines and consider their practice as a response to God's love.

### Stewardship
#### A Way of Living

Great News! Stewardship is not about money! At least not *just* about money. Certainly, stewardship relates to money, and, yes, we need to tithe. However, stewardship branches out into multiple areas of life. Properly practiced, this act of service can lead to peace and purpose in living.

## The Ten Commandments

When the Ten Commandments are in the news, it is usually because a judge or teacher has hung them up on the walls. The Ten Commandments do not need to be posted or even preached nearly so much as they need to be practiced and viewed as life-giving, joyful affirmations of a better way of life.

## What Would Jesus Say?
### A Lenten Study

To address what Jesus would say, we need to discover what Jesus did say. These lessons will attempt to help us understand Jesus' teachings and apply them today.

**NextSunday Studies**
**are available from**

Manufactured by Amazon.ca
Bolton, ON

10233476R00048